AF585260

AUSTRALIA'S ENDANGERED ANIMALS ...AND THEIR HABITATS

A FOCUS ON ALPINE HABITATS

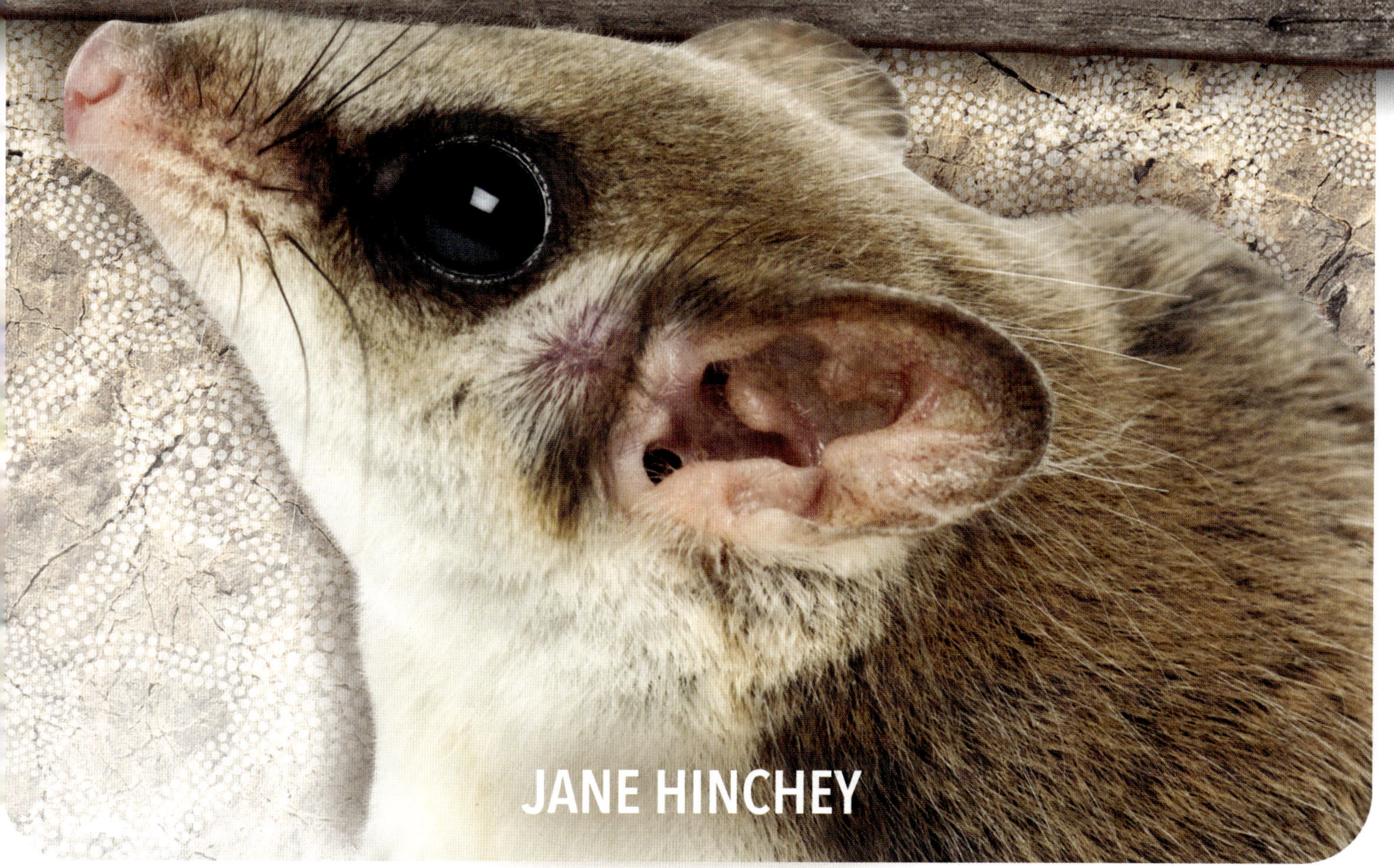

JANE HINCHEY

Redback Publishing
PO Box 357 Frenchs Forest NSW 2086
Australia

www.redbackpublishing.com.au
orders@redbackpublishing.com.au

ISBN 978-1-925630-72-5

Author: Jane Hinchey
Editor: Michael Anderson
Designer: Redback Publishing

Original illustrations © Redback Publishing 2019
Originated by Redback Publishing

Printed and bound in China

Acknowledgements
Abbreviations: l–left, r–right, b–bottom, t–top, c–centre, m–middle
We would like to thank the following for permission to reproduce photographs: (Images © shutterstock)
p5 By I, Beentree (Kookaburra Eggs), p13br By John Tann, p15tr By IgorGolovniov, p20m By Magnus Kjaergaard, p21tl By Catching The Eye, p22t By Photo by Phil Spark, p24ml By IgorGolovniov, p25tl By Canley - Own work CC BY-SA 4.0, p28bl By Codman at English, p30t By simona flamigni.

A catalogue record for this book is available from the National Library of Australia

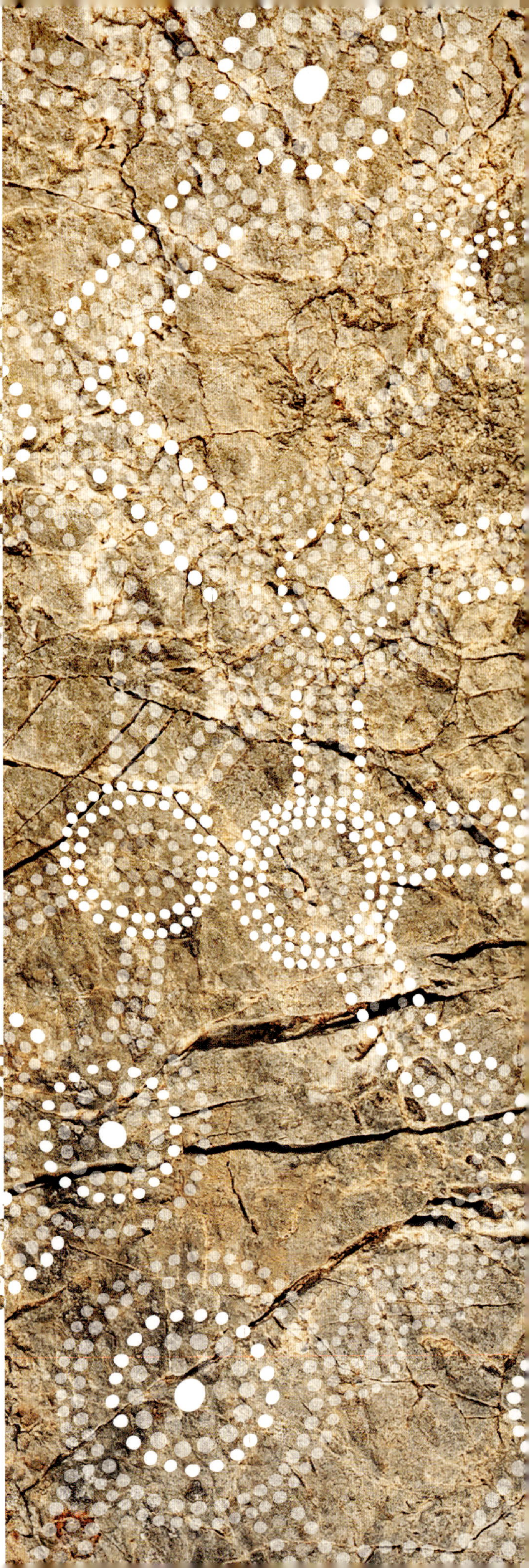

CONTENTS

Australia is unique. It is not only a country and an island, but also one of the world's seven continents. Australia was cut off from the rest of the world's landmass for over 100 million years, which allowed for a diverse range of animals to flourish. It is home to more than one million species of plants and animals, many of which are found nowhere else in the world, and less than half have been described scientifically. About 85 per cent of plants, 84 per cent of mammals, 45 per cent of birds, 88 per cent of reptiles and 94 per cent of amphibians are endemic. In Australia there are more than 378 species of mammals, 828 species of birds, 300 species of lizards, 140 species of snakes and two species of crocodiles.

FABULOUS FAUNA

Among Australia's best-known animals are the kangaroo, koala, echidna, platypus, wallaby and wombat.

AUSTRALIA ANIMAL CLASSIFICATION CHART

Scientists classify animals into groups in order to study and understand them. Each group can have numerous sub-groups. Australia's animals are divided into six major groups.

Group	Characteristics	Examples
AMPHIBIAN	Lives on both land and water Has smooth skin, webbed feet Lays eggs	Frogs such as the spotted tree frog and corroboree frog
BIRD	Hatches from eggs Has feathers and wings	Australian bustard, cassowary, kookaburra
FISH	Lives in water Hatch from soft eggs Has fins and scales	Fish such as the Eastern freshwater cod, Australian smelt and estuary perch
MAMMAL	Warm blooded Lactate to feed young Most have body hair	Koala, wombat, kangaroo, wallaby, possum
REPTILE	Hatches from eggs Lives on land Has scales	Eastern bearded dragon, eastern brown snake, freshwater crocodile
INVERTEBRATES	No backbone Many forms of locomotion	Beetles, flies, mosquitoes, snails, worms, crabs, squid and spiders such as the redback spider

SPOTTED TREE FROG

KOOKABURRA EGGS

BBER FISH

WOMBAT

EASTERN BEARDED DRAGON

REDBACK SPIDER

DID YOU KNOW?

Aboriginal people have a multifaceted classification system for organising knowledge, which includes the animal kingdom. This system is highly complex and includes regional, cultural and spiritual influences, as well as practical considerations such as if an animal is edible, and whether it is poisonous.

UNIQUE AUSTRALIAN HABITATS

A habitat is a place that provides shelter, safety, food and water for the animals that live there. The creatures and plants all do things to help keep the whole habitat healthy and in balance, and rely upon each other for their survival. Animals like cockroaches eat the dead plants and recycle the nutrients back into the soil, which helps the plants to grow. Bats, birds and insects help spread seeds. Every plant and creature serves a purpose.

Australia is a large country with many different climates that has contributed to its range of habitats. These habitats extend from Antarctica to the tropics, encompassing environments as diverse as oceans and coasts, mangroves and rivers, coastal heathlands, mountain forests and rainforests, alpine meadows, woodlands and the dry grasslands of the interior. Each habitat can also include smaller habitats within it. For example, there may be a lush waterhole in a desert environment.

Australia's unique habitats are under threat from urban and agricultural development, fishing, trawling and harvesting fossil fuels. Australia's increasing rate of destruction of native vegetation - nearly 300,000 hectares per year - further endangers nearly 1,800 threatened species. Australia is amongst the world's worst countries for deforestation.

Freshwater Habitats include rivers, lakes, billabongs and ponds. They support animals such as the eastern water skink, dragonfly, platypus, the Macquarie perch and yellow-spotted bell frog.

Australia's coastline measures 36,700 kilometres and is home to the majority of the population. **Coastal and Ocean Habitats** encompass more than just the country's long sandy beaches and offshore islands and reefs. There are also a diverse array of sub-habitats from mangroves, lakes and river estuaries, to rocky headlands and granite coastline. Also included are the fertile plains between the Great Dividing Range and the sea. Each of these areas supports coastal and marine life, which is impacted by any changing environmental conditions.

Desert Habitats include savannah grasslands, low woodlands and shrublands, sandy and rocky areas and tall shrub areas. These areas support animals such as the bilby, the thorny devil and the bearded dragon.

About 70 per cent of mainland Australia, approximately 5.3 million square kilometres, is arid and semi-arid, while 18 per cent is desert. Australia's desert mammals have suffered a very high extinction rate, with animals such as the lesser bilby and desert rat kangaroo gone forever.

Tundra, Ice and Snow Habitats range from the Alpine mountains and forests of the Snowy Mountains, to Australian Antarctic Territory. Antarctic animals include sea lions and whales, krill, penguins and squid.

Australia recognises over 900 wetlands for their national importance.

Wetland Habitats include arid and alpine, inland to coastal ecosystems. Forested wetlands include mangrove forests, river red gum forests and casuarina swamps. Animals such as the northern corroboree frog, Australian pelican and pig-nosed turtle live there. Australia's wetlands are vital for many migratory birds.

Australia's cities and towns are **Urban Habitats** and include areas such as parks, gardens, ports and harbours, rivers and buildings where animals like the grey headed flying fox, Eastern water skink and Australian magpie call home.

Australia's **Alpine Habitats** range from grasslands to forests and support animals such as the broad-toothed rat, Kosciuszko grasshopper and the mountain pygmy-possum.

TURN OVER FOR MORE ON AUSTRALIA'S AMAZING ALPINE HABITATS

Rainforest in Australia have been divided into four broad groups: **hot dry** in the north, **hot moist** in the northeast and both **warm dry** and **cool moist** in the southeast. Australia's Wet Tropics World Heritage Area in northeastern Queensland includes both mountain ranges covered in rainforests and lowland tropical rainforests. The Daintree is home to some of the rarest and most spectacular flora and fauna in the world. It is a complex web of diverse habitats, with creatures living at all levels of the forest, from the canopy to under the forest floor. Some of the creatures found in the rainforests include the Ulysses butterfly, the Boyd's forest dragon and the endangered southern cassowary, with only 1,200 left in Australia.

Australia's **Dry Forests and Woodlands** support animals such as the brush-tailed phascogale, squirrel glider and regent honeyeater. Dry forests are not as tall as rainforests.

FOCUS ON ALPINE HABITATS

Australia's alpine environment is small but spectacular. The mountain ranges have formed over 600 million years and are older than the European Alps and the Himalayas. The Australian Alps cover 15,000-square kilometres and include nine national parks.

Over 54 per cent of Australia's alpine area is in New South Wales, while the rest is in Victoria and the Australian Capital Territory. Despite the greater part of the region being in New South Wales, it still only occupies 0.54 per cent of the state. It is the smallest bioregion in New South Wales and one of the smallest in Australia.

Australia's main alpine and subalpine areas are in:

- The Snowy Mountains in New South Wales
- The Bogong High Plains in Victoria
- Central and southwestern Tasmania

HISTORY HUNTER

Aboriginal people have inhabited the area for at least 21,000 years and also used the alps as an annual meeting place during Bogong moth season, which they used as a food source. The black possum, platypus, raven and eagle also have special significance.

The Snowy Mountains

Predominantly alpine and subalpine mountainous areas and tablelands, the Snowy Mountains boasts Australia's highest peak Mt Kosciuszko, which reaches a height of 2,228 metres above sea level. Kosciuszko National Park is the largest national park in New South Wales and features mountain peaks, grasslands, alpine lakes and granite boulders. The range is also known for the Snowy Mountains Scheme, a project to dam the Snowy River, providing both water for irrigation and hydro-electricity. Many rare or endangered plant and animal species occur within the Snowy Mountains. 34 threatened fauna species have been recorded in the area, including 10 mammals, 16 birds, 5 amphibians and 3 reptiles. The Australian Alps are on the National Heritage List and protected by federal law.

Alpine Wetlands

There are many alpine wetlands in Australia that provide a habitat for rare and endangered plants and animals. Blue Lake in Kosciusko National Park, New South Wales was formed around 15,000 years ago and is one of only four glacial lakes in Australia. It is home to mountain galaxias, the only native fish found above the snowline in winter.

Tasmania's Alpine Region

Alpine and subalpine areas occupy about 3 per cent of Tasmania's land surface, but they are rich with flora and fauna species found nowhere else in the world. Many of these are endemic. Much of Tasmania's alpine zone can be found on mountains in the western half of the state. Four out of the five highest mountains in Tasmania are in the Cradle Mountain-Lake St Clair National Park. Part of the Tasmanian Wilderness World Heritage Area, the park boasts a diverse array of habitats, from rugged mountains, to glacial lakes and streams and ancient pines.

Bogs and Fens

Bogs and fens are common in Australia's alpine regions. There is over 9,000 acres of Sphagnum shrub bog in Kosciuszko National Park compared to the 6,700 acres of bog in alpine Victoria and over 7,000 acres of Sphagnum moss communities occurring above 800 metres in Tasmania. These areas preserve peat and provide significant habitat for a number of endemic and threatened animal species. These include the southern and northern Corroboree frogs, the Baw Baw frog, the alpine tree frog, the alpine she-oak skink and the alpine bog skink.

FACT BOX

Major rivers such as the Murray, the Murrumbidgee and the Snowy all begin in the Alps.

1800

1400

1100

Altitude in Metres

ALPINE AREA

above 1,800 to 1,850 metres

Alpine areas are on mountains above the tree zone, meaning the point where it is too cold for trees to grow. In Australia, the tree line starts about 1,800 to 1,850 metres above sea level.

Compared to many other countries, Australia doesn't have very tall mountains so only has a small alpine area. In total, the land above 1,850 metres is less than 80 square kilometres. Snow lies on Australia's highest mountains for about 120 days each year.

Alpine areas encompass a range of habitats, including:

- Grasslands
- Heathlands
- Bogs and swamp areas
- Rocky slopes and boulders.

Tall alpine heathlands and herbfields dominate the high alpine landscape. About 200 species of plants, such as prickly snow grass and alpine wallaby grass, are found in the alpine areas. Sphagnum sedges and heath grow at alpine bogs and alpine marsh marigold grows in areas below the snowdrift. A high percentage of alpine species are endemic.

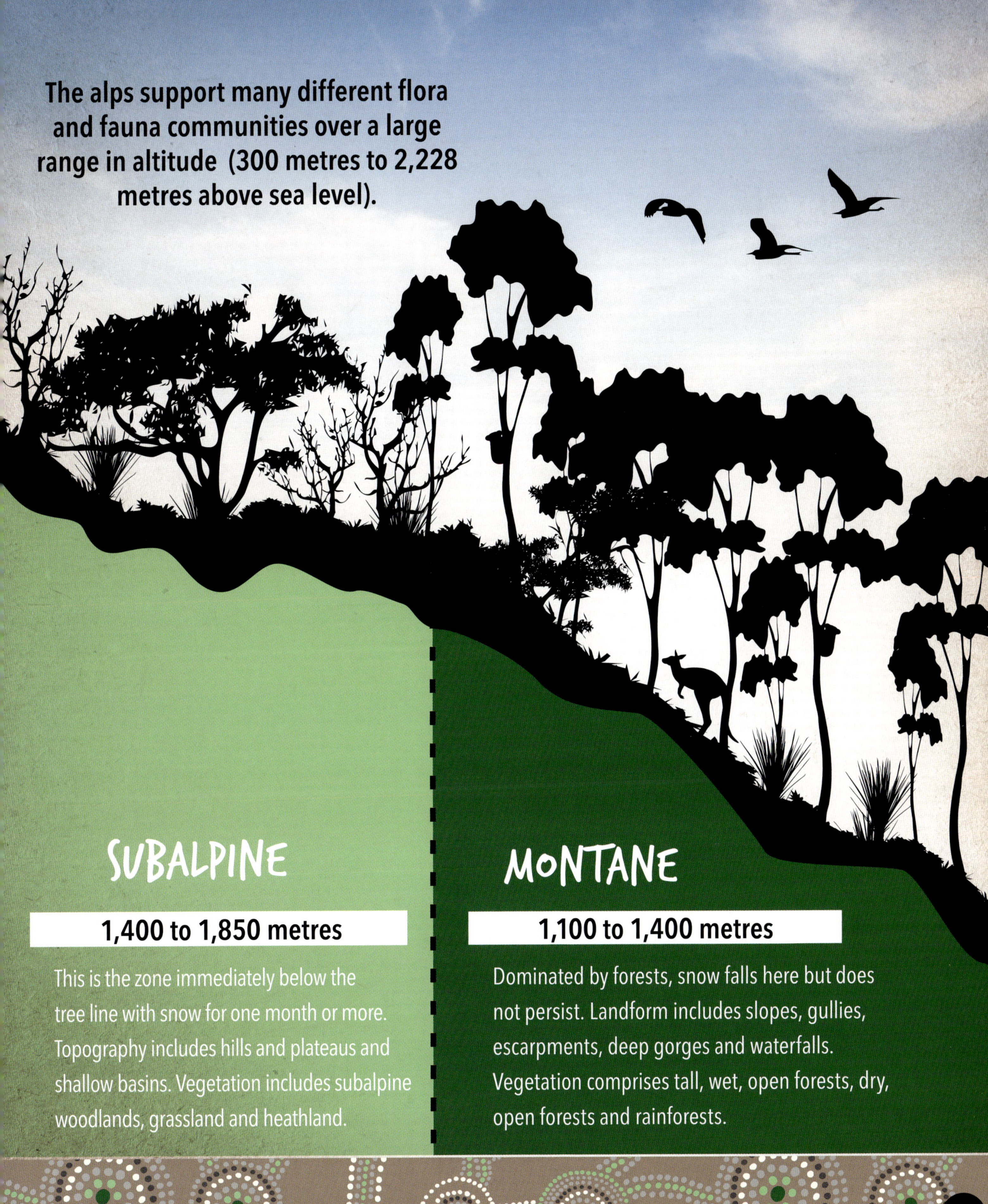
The alps support many different flora and fauna communities over a large range in altitude (300 metres to 2,228 metres above sea level).
SUBALPINE
1,400 to 1,850 metres
This is the zone immediately below the tree line with snow for one month or more. Topography includes hills and plateaus and shallow basins. Vegetation includes subalpine woodlands, grassland and heathland.
MONTANE
1,100 to 1,400 metres
Dominated by forests, snow falls here but does not persist. Landform includes slopes, gullies, escarpments, deep gorges and waterfalls. Vegetation comprises tall, wet, open forests, dry, open forests and rainforests.

AMAZING ALPINE ANIMALS

More than 40 species of native mammals, 200 bird species, 30 reptiles species, 15 amphibians, 14 native fish species and many species of invertebrates occur in the Australian Alps.

LEADBEATER'S POSSUM

Mammals

Mammals such as the eastern grey kangaroo, common wombat, swamp wallaby and red-neck wallaby, common possum and Leadbeater's possum are found in the forests and woodlands of the montane section of the alps. The only mammal found in the subalpine and alpine areas is the mountain pygmy possum.

Birds

No birds live all year round in alpine areas, however birds such as the gang-gang cockatoo, the grey fantail, the crimson rosella, the fan-tailed cuckoo, the emu, the superb lyrebird and the yellow-faced honeyeater are seen in the grasslands and forests in summer. Birds such as the grey currawong, the Australian kestrel, the Australian pipit, the white-browed scrub-wren, the flame robin, the pied currawong and the little raven are seen at higher elevations. Less than half the species of birds found in the summer months stay during winter.

AUSTRALIAN PIPIT

COPPERHEAD SNAKE

Reptiles

Distribution of reptiles depends on temperature and basking sites, as they regulate their body temperature by basking in the sun. Some reptiles that occur in the region are the grass skink, the water skink, the copperhead snake and the southern blue tongue. The alpine water skink and she-oak skink are also found at higher altitudes.

ADAPTATIONS, HIBERNATION AND TORPOR

Many animals have adapted to the freezing alpine winters by shutting down their metabolism and hibernating or going into torpor, which is a short-term reduction of body temperature on cool days induced by a seasonal trigger. The mountain pygmy possum hibernates during the coldest part of the season. Many reptiles and amphibians become inactive.

Disrupting the Alpine Food Web

When one species is threatened the complex habitat and food web it is a part of also becomes threatened. A food chain is a sequence of which animals eat what food, while the food web links all the food chains together. The food web from Australia's alpine habitats encompass many species from tiny plants to larger animals. While an owl might not eat a plant species directly, it could feed on the animals that do. When one link in the food chain or web is threatened, it puts the entire ecosystem in danger.

Wildlife WARRIOR

Can you name three different habitats near where you live? What animals live there?

CLASSIFICATION AND IDENTIFICATION

Australia has the worst mammal extinction rate in the world. Globally, one out of three mammal extinctions in the last 400 years has occurred in Australia. Furthermore, over 1,700 plant and animal species are listed as threatened with extinction.

There are thousands of fauna species living in Australia's different habitats, with new species being discovered every year. The use of an international classification system is extremely important.

When identifying characteristics that make a species vulnerable, the international classification system used is overseen by the International Union for the Conservation of Nature (IUCN) red list.

The International Union for Conservation of Nature

Many factors are used to assess the conservation status of a species. The International Union for Conservation of Nature is the global authority on the status of the natural world and the actions needed to protect it. The IUCN gathers data about different species from a huge range of sources, such as biologists, conservationists and statisticians.

The IUCN Red List of Threatened Species is recognised globally as the authority on the status of endangered animals. It divides species into nine different categories:

- Extinct (EX)
- Extinct in the Wild (EW)
- Critically Endangered (CR)
- Endangered (EN)
- Vulnerable (VU)
- Near Threatened (NT)
- Least Concern (LC)
- Data Deficient (DD)
- Not Evaluated (NE)

Species in the Critically Endangered, Endangered and Vulnerable categories are all considered 'threatened.'

In Australia, animals are classified at both State and Federal levels. At Federal level the current categories are:

- Extinct
- Extinct in the Wild
- Critically Endangered
- Endangered
- Vulnerable
- Conservation Dependent

EXTINCT ANIMALS

Extinction is when every single member of a species dies and none are left alive. Scientists go to great lengths to determine that a species is extinct – a process that begins with careful monitoring of the species while it still exists.

Since European settlement, 24 birds, 7 frogs and 27 mammal species or subspecies have become extinct in Australia.

TASMANIAN WOLF

Classification

There are many ways to classify species. We can choose any characteristic as a basis for sorting animals. These may include body form, colour pattern, mode of development or genetics. Classification helps organise the differences within and between groups of animals. Classification of animals helps identify them, understand them, quantify the threat to them and take steps to conserve a species.

WHAT IS THE PROBLEM?

Why are so many of Australia's species under threat? There are a number of major issues impacting native animals.

Changing Ecosystems

An animal's survival often depends on the animal's ecosystem maintaining balance. Any change to the ecosystem can impact the species living there. One example of this is the food chain. The loss of the smallest creature can impact the larger creatures that feed off them, all the way to the top of the food chain. These interconnected food webs are an essential part of the overall ecosystem.

Climate Change

Climate change is affecting, and will continue to affect habitats in numerous ways including directly altered weather and rainfall patterns. These events could disrupt the normal cycle of variability to which animals and plants have adapted. Climate change impacts the amount of rain in arid areas and cause more erosion when heavier rains occur. Temperature changes will also increase the size and timing of bushfires. In Alpine areas a change in temperature means trees might grow at higher altitudes, which changes entire ecosystems.

Habitat Destruction

Australia's animal habitats are impacted by development. Land has been cleared for agriculture and for roads and ski resorts.

FIRE MANAGEMENT

Fires are a natural and vital part of the Australian landscape that bring forth new plant growth and food for the species that live there. Aboriginal people have practiced managed fires for thousands of years but since European settlement, the pattern of burning has changed. Because of this, bushfires are now more frequent and usually more damaging than before, which has directly impacted native animals. Only recently have governments been working with the traditional Aboriginal custodians of different areas to reintroduce controlled burning, which helps expand the population of many different species.

Habitat Degradation

There are many ways in which habitat loss can impact the animals that live there.

- Habitat loss can wipe out all the species that live in one area.
- Habitat fragmentation makes it difficult for animals to move from one area to another, as they normally would.
- Habitat alteration, such as the loss of understorey shrubs, logs, food plants and old trees with hollows means that animals don't have protection, feeding and nesting areas.

Other primary factors causing this loss of wildlife include:

- Introduced plants and weeds
- Introduced animal species such as feral foxes, cats, dogs, pigs, goats, rabbits, donkeys, horses, camels, buffalo and feral cattle
- Removal of Aboriginal people from their native lands has had a devastating impact on these environments
- Clearing native vegetation
- Changes in fire regimes and an increase in the extent and severity of wildfires
- Agriculture and grazing
- Hunting
- Tourism and four-wheel drive damage
- Disease
- Deforestation

FERAL ANIMALS

Native animals are under threat from more than humans. Feral animals introduced to the country now cause havoc with native animal populations. The major pest animals in Snowy River Shire are dingoes and wild dogs, feral pigs, foxes, rabbits and wild deer. Feral cats, feral goats and horses are thought to also be a problem.

Rabbits

Europeans brought rabbits to Australia for food and to be used for hunting. The rabbits quickly bred and spread and have caused considerable damage to the natural environment.

It is estimated that there are now 200 million rabbits in Australia, competing with native animals for food and shelter. In 2016, there was evidence that rabbits had moved above the snow line in the alps.

Pigs

Feral pigs are found in a variety of habitats including subalpine grasslands and forests. Along with feral deer, pigs are believed to do more damage than horses to alpine streams.

Feral Cats

Cats are not native to Australia. They arrived with European settlement and are now considered to be a major threat to Australia's native animals. Feral cats are different to domestic cats and stray cats in that they live and reproduce in the wild and survive by hunting or scavenging. They have no need for humans. Feral cats cover 99.8 per cent of Australia, including on the highest alpine peaks. It's estimated feral cats eat 75 million native animals a night – more than 20 billion mammals, reptiles, birds and even insects every year.

HORSES

Australia has the largest wild horse population of any country in the world. Horses arrived in Australia with the First Fleet in 1788. By 1804, some horses had escaped from farms and were roaming wild. Later, many former work horses were set free when cars and motorised farm machines arrived. Today, herds of wild brumbies are found right across the Australian mainland, including from the highest to lowest elevations in the Australian Alps.

Why Are They a Problem?

Horses are heavy and have hard hooves. Their hooves destroy vegetation and damage riverbanks. They wear tracks in the soil, causing erosion and can destroy the burrows of animals as they can walk over them. Horses also compete with native animals for grass.

Not everyone believes the brumbies are a problem. Some experts say that horses have achieved an ecological balance with their habitat. But the general consensus is that they are having a negative impact on the alpine environment and need to be dealt with.

What is Being Done About Them?

There is a proposal to trap and domesticate or euthanise more than 1,000 horses in the alpine region. The culling of brumbies is a contentious topic and many people continue to oppose it. The New South Wales government is considering a protection plan as an alternative position.

HORSES IN AUSSIE FOLKLORE

The Man from Snowy River **by 'Banjo' Paterson is one of Australia's most well-known poems. Many Australians see wild horses as a part of the country's bush culture and history.**

ENDANGERED MAMMALS

Australia's alpine regions are home to many unique species. Each animal is extremely important in maintaining the balance in its ecosystem and a loss of any species impacts the whole alpine food web. Nearly half Australia's unique mammal species are either extinct or threatened with extinction, with land clearing and habitat destruction being a major reason for this. In alpine regions, forestry and the building of ski resorts has been a major issue.

BROAD-TOOTHED RATS

STATUS: Vulnerable

FEATURES: A gentle, medium sized native rat with a broad face, short tail and stocky body.

ABOUT: Their diet consists of grass and sedge stems, seeds and moss spores. The female has two or three young in summer. They use runways in the snow to move around.

HABITAT: Broad-toothed rats live in alpine and subalpine heaths, grasslands, woodlands and wet sedge of mainland Australia and Tasmania. They build nests of grass in understory or under logs, huddling together in winter.

MAIN THREATS: The broad-toothed rat was nearly wiped out in 2003 when bushfires destroyed its habitat in areas of Namadgi National Park. However numbers have risen again as the habitat has recovered. Other threats include climate change and feral animals.

FUN FACT: Broad-toothed Rats are like a native 'guinea-pig' in appearance and character.

SMOKY MOUSE

STATUS: Critically Endangered

ABOUT: The Smoky Mouse is similar in size to a small rat. It has soft pale-grey to bluish-grey fur with paler belly and dark hair around the eyes. The feet are light pink and the ears a grey-pink. Females produce one to two litters of three to four young a year. Colonies of one male and several females live together in burrows. The mice do not usually live longer than two years. Their diet consists of Bogong moths, berries and seeds.

HABITAT: Occurs in regions up to 1,800 metres, mostly in sclerophyll forest, heathland and open forest. Distribution is limited to a small number of sites in western, southern and eastern Victoria, southeast New South Wales and the Australian Capital Territory.

MAIN THREATS: Loss of habitat due to timber harvesting and road building, altered fire regimes, dieback caused by the cinnamon fungus, climate change and feral animals.

FUN FACT: Scientists have bolstered the numbers of the smoky mouse using flowers and food in breeding enclosures of six adult mice.

NUMBERS: Fewer than 1,000 left in Australia. There are only about 100 recorded in the wild.

ENDANGERED SPECIES AREA

Indicator Species

The smoky mouse is considered an indicator species, which means that any information learnt about it is used to give researchers a greater understanding of the survival of other species in the area.

SHARING IS NOT CARING

Many native animals have to compete for food and shelter with introduced animals such as rabbitsts and cattle.

ANIMALS IN FOCUS

The Mountain Pygmy Possum

CONSERVATION STATUS (IUCN): Critically Endangered

CONSERVATION STATUS (FEDERAL): Endangered

This small marsupial has grey brown fur on top, with lighter fur underneath and dark patches around its eyes. It feeds on Bogong moths during spring and summer, then fruits and other insects when the Bogong moths die or return to Queensland. In winter, the mountain pygmy possum hibernates, the only marsupial that does so.

Males and females live separately, with the female occupying the best habitat areas. Breeding happens quickly in spring, with females having a litter of up to four and the young being weaned about ten weeks after birth. Generally they live up to three years, although females have been known to live twelve years.

Unlike most other possums, it is mainly ground-dwelling, inhabiting alpine and subalpine boulderfields in south-eastern Australia. There are approximately 2,600 mountain pygmy possums left, living in only three known populations: Mount Higginbotham and Mount Buller in Victoria, and Kosciuszko National Park in New South Wales.

FUN FACT
The Mountain Pygmy Possum is the only Australian mammal adapted to live exclusively in the alpine zone.

MAJOR THREATS TO THE MOUNTAIN PYGMY POSSUM:

- Degradation, fragmentation and loss of habitat due to ski resort developments
- Climate change impacts this species by bringing them out of hibernation before their main food source, the Bogong moth arrives
- Predators such as foxes and cats

What is Being Done to Save Them?

A national recovery plan was drafted in 2010 to ensure the mountain pygmy possum's survival, which included a number of captive breeding programs and research. In the past three years, numbers of the possum has risen.

Exciting News!

A new population of mountain pygmy possums was recently discovered below the tree line in Kosciuszko National Park. Finding the possums in this new habitat will help in understanding how this species will adapt to future challenges.

MEALTIME FOR THE MOUNTAIN PYGMY POSSUM

Bogong moths travel over 1,500 km during their lifetime of a year. Every spring, they fly south from QLD to spend the heat of summer in alpine caves. Some alpine caves have a thick carpet of dead moth bodies built up from countless generations. After summer, the Bogong moth returns to QLD to breed.

ROAD SAFETY!

Mount Hotham resort cuts across a path taken by male mountain pygmy possums during breeding season. To ensure the possums remained safe, a tunnel was dug under the road. Male possums use this tunnel to go in search of females.

FROGS IN DANGER

Australia has over 200 species of frog, but the populations are declining. Fifteen species are currently endangered, twelve are listed as vulnerable and four have become extinct.

The seven most at-risk frogs are:

- The southern corroboree frog
- The northern corroboree frog
- The Baw Baw frog
- The spotted tree frog
- The Tasmanian tree frog
- The Kroombit tinker frog
- The armoured mist frog

Most Australian alpine frogs are listed as rare or endangered.

CORROBORREE FROGS

There are two species of corroborree frog – the northern and southern corroborree Frog. Both are endangered. They are small, brightly coloured, ground dwelling frogs that secrete a toxin poisonous to predators.

The black and yellow southern corroborree frog is found in a small part of the subalpine area of Kosciuszko National Park. It breeds in summer and their eggs hatch in autumn or early winter and the tadpoles enter the pools in sphagnum bogs. They take three to five years to mature and can live for up to nine years.

The southern corroborree frog is adapted for cooler temperatures, so climate change in the alps, and the advent of hotter weather has already impacted it. It is thought that there are fewer than 100 of these frogs left in the wild.

The southern corroboree Frog is listed as Critically Endangered on the IUCN Red List.

It is also listed as Critically Endangered nationally, and Endangered in New South Wales.

BAW BAW FROG

This unusual amphibian has adapted to extremely cold, high-altitude habitats. Found only on the Mt Baw Baw plateau in Victoria, the Baw Baw frog has suffered a decline in numbers due to habitat destruction, deforestation and ski resorts and climate change. An infectious disease called chytrid fungus has also decimated the population of this small, brown frog, leading to a 92 per cent decline in numbers since 2006.

Baw Baw Frogs are carnivores, feeding on insects, worms and other invertebrates. These frogs live underground and are probably inactive during the coldest months when the plateau is covered in snow and breed between September and December. They can live up to 14 years.

Baw Baw Frogs are Critically Endangered. Fewer than 250 are left in a tiny area of about ten square kilometres. There is now a breeding program at Melbourne Zoo that aims to save this small frog from extinction.

ALPINE TREE FROG

The alpine tree frog is the only tree frog known to occur above the winter snowline on mainland Australia. It is a small tree frog, growing to about three centimetres long, and can be green, brown or grey, with dark striped markings. They feed on beetles, spiders, flies and moth larvae and breed in December.

The alpine tree frog is found in a variety of habitats including woodland, grassland, heath and herb fields, generally above 1,100 metres. Ozone depletion is a likely reason for the decline in numbers, with the frogs suffering due to increased exposure to ultra-violet (UV) radiation.

The alpine tree frog is listed as Vulnerable under the Commonwealth Environment Protection and Biodiversity Conservation Act 1999. It is listed as Endangered in New South Wales.

MAIN THREATS TO FROGS:

- Loss of wetland areas and damage to breeding sites
- The conversion of ponds and waterholes to dams for stock use. This results in cattle destroying their habitat.
- Fungus and disease
- The forestry industry
- Tourism
- Pollution
- Climate change
- Chemicals and insecticides from agriculture polluting water
- Introduction of fish that prey on frog eggs and tadpoles
- Other predators
- Most frogs are salt intolerant, so a major issue is increased salinity

WHY DON'T WE CARE MORE?

Why are some endangered animals more popular than others? Why have we heard of China's giant panda, but never heard of Australia's own Critically Endangered tinkling frog? The northern hairy nosed wombat may look better on a poster than the Lord Howe Island phasmid, but both are important Australian species.

Here are three creatures it's time you heard of. Perhaps you can put their image on a poster.

Glossy Skink

The glossy skink is a ground dwelling lizard that lives in Tasmania's swamps and wetlands vegetation and in alpine and high montane regions in the Canberra region. It has a glossy brown body with a dark vertebral strip. The males are smaller than females. In Tasmania it has a scattered distribution on the east coast, north coast, inland near Cradle Mountain and Cape Barren Island. Threats to the skink include habitat destruction and degradation due to urban encroachment, forestry and agriculture. Also alterations to water flow and water quality. The alpine skinks are quite susceptible to local extinction through big catastrophic events, such as wildfires.

A similar skink is the rare glossy grass skink (mountain bog skink) found in a restricted area in Kosciusko National Park.

Murray Crayfish

The Murray crayfish is the second largest freshwater crayfish in the world. They live in parts of the Murray River and the Murrumbidgee River and in some dams. The female crayfish lays 500 to 1,000 eggs once a year and carries them under her tail as both eggs and when they hatch. They are long living and can live for up to 50 years. Major threats include changes to their habitat, especially water flow when dams and weirs are built.

The Shaw Galaxias

The Shaw Galaxias is a small native freshwater fish and the only native fish recorded from above 800 metres in the Macalister River system in the Alpine National Park. This Critically Endangered alpine fish was on the verge of extinction when scientists and government agencies banded together to remove introduced trout from their environment. More than 700 trout were removed from the creek where the Shaw Galaxias was found and a barrier to make the trout move downstream installed. So far this has successfully saved the Shaw Galaxias from extinction.

BIRDS UNDER THREAT

Australia's alpine habitats are home to a wide range of birds, both endemic and migratory. There are 828 species of Australian native birds and nearly half are endemic. More than 80 per cent of Australia's parrots are found only in Australia and the country also boasts the highest diversity of honeyeaters in the world. 16 bird species found in the Snowy River Shire are endangered.

The Powerful Owl

The powerful owl is the largest of Australia's owls and endemic to eastern and southeastern Australia's forests and woodlands. They are carnivorous, eating small marsupials and rabbits. The powerful owl mates for life, sometimes for over 30 years. They are listed as vulnerable in New South Wales and endangered in Victoria. Their main threats are due to clearing of its habitat, including hollow trees.

Swift Parrots

Swift parrots are one of Australia's most endangered birds. They are a colourful, medium-sized parrot with a green body, dark blue crown and crimson throat and a long pointed purple-red tail. They have been severely impacted by the clearing of the forests and woodlands where they live. Deforestation in Tasmania has also made them vulnerable to being eaten by sugar gliders.

FEATHERED FACT FILE

Since colonisation, nine bird species have become extinct. A further 50 are under threat or endangered. Millions of birds are killed each year as a result of deforestation and loss of habitat. Feral cats kill over one million birds a day, or 377 million birds annually.

THE MURRAY RIVER

Forty kilometres from Mount Kosciusko lies the source of Australia's greatest river, the Murray River. This iconic river rises from three springs at Forest Hill and then flows for another 2,225 kilometres to South Australia and the sea.

The Murray River is part of the Murray–Darling Basin, Australia's largest river system, covering over a million square kilometres in southeastern Australia, or 14 per cent of the country's landmass. Its diverse landscapes and complex ecosystems include over 30,000 wetlands and 77,000 kilometres of rivers. It includes not only the Murray River and Darling River, but also many other rivers, creeks, lakes and waterways. The Murray River represents the border between New South Wales and Victoria.

ABORIGINAL CULTURE

The Murray Cod plays an important role in Aboriginal culture. Stories tell of a huge Murray cod forming the Murray River.

Murray Cod

A MIGHTY COD

The largest recorded Murray cod was 1.8m long and weighed 113kg!

IUCN STATUS: Critically Endangered
ENVIRONMENTAL PROTECTION OF BIODIVERSITY AND CONSERVATION ACT: Vulnerable

The Murray Cod is Australia's largest native freshwater fish. The cod has a cream to white belly and green mottled pattern on the body and head. It has a large mouth and rounded tail. It's a long-lived fish and one cod was aged at 48 years. It is carnivorous, feeding on other fish.

Numbers in the Murray River have severely depleted. Commercial overfishing in the late 1800s severely depleted the Murray cod population. While this commercial fishing is now banned, recreational overfishing is still an issue, including in the high country. Other threats include loss of and changes to habitats, dams and river blackwater events that cause the cod to suffocate.

In 2010, a Murray Cod Recovery Program was prepared. The aim is to expand the cod population to 60 per cent of pre-European settlement numbers by 2060.

WHAT IS BEING DONE TO SAVE AUSTRALIA'S ENDANGERED SPECIES?

The Department of the Environment and Heritage administers *Australia's Endangered Species Protection Act.* Recovery projects study and conserve threatened species and their habitats, including plants, reptiles, amphibians, invertebrates, fish, mammals and birds.

Every state and territory has a conservation agency, which is involved in looking after habitats and management of species, including threatened species.

Organisations such as botanic gardens, zoos and universities are funded by state and federal governments to look after and research endangered animals. Some are trying to breed threatened species.

The Australian Government has established a new national approach to threatened species, which includes:

- tackling feral cats
- establishing safe havens for species most at risk
- emergency interventions to avert extinctions

Most endangered animals have a recovery plan to ensure the species' survival.

Feral Cats

The government is currently testing new baiting methods for feral cats with the aim of culling up to 2 million of them. Animal rights groups oppose this as barbaric.

LEARNING FROM AUSTRALIA'S FIRST PEOPLE

Today, scientists work with Indigenous communities to better understand and maintain Australia's different environments and habitats that Aboriginal people have successfully maintained for tens of thousands of years.

Aboriginal rangers are a vital part of protecting Australia's native species. These rangers understand their country and the species in it. Indigenous Rangers undertake valuable environmental work across a diverse range of Australian habitats. Some of the significant work these rangers do is remove invasive animals and weeds, monitor biodiversity, revegetate and restore natural landscapes, deal with injured animals and use fire management to promote regrowth and biodiversity. Over 70 per cent of ranger groups work to protect threatened species across Australia.

In the Snowy Mountains

In 2016, after a decade of negotiation, The New South Wales government signed a memorandum of understanding (MOU) with the Monaro Ngarigo people that solidifies the local Indigenous community's role in preserving the park's cultural value and advising on matters such as fire management, feral animals and tourism.

ABORIGINAL PEOPLE AND THE AUSTRALIAN ALPS

"The Mountains are very old and an ongoing life force that strengthens the ancestral link of our people. We have a living, spiritual connection with the mountains. We retain family stories and memories of the mountains, which makes them spiritually and culturally significant to us. Our traditional knowledge and cultural practices still exist and need to be maintained...

Our people travelled from many directions over long distances to gather peacefully on the mountains for trade, ceremony, marriages, social events and to settle differences.

The cycle of life and many seasons influence the movement of our people through the mountains to the sea and the desert. The stars, clouds, sun and the moon guided people to and from places of importance. These travel routes continue to be used and spoken about today...

Let us not forget the past while we look forward to the future. Past and present practices make us strong and we are committed to making this a better country for all."

Extracts from: *Kosciuszko National Park 2006, Plan of Management', A Statement from the Kosciuszko Aboriginal Working Group*, p. xi.

WHAT CAN YOU DO?

- Never dump a pet in the wild. They can survive and wreak havoc with native species. Take unwanted pets to the RSPCA.
- If you have a cat, attach a bell to its collar. Make sure it does not catch native birds or other animals.
- When fishing, do not lose any fishing line or hooks.
- Use less energy and use green energy where possible. The more sustainable your life is, the less you are contributing to climate change.
- Cut back on chemical use. Household, garden and agricultural chemicals end up in our river systems and ultimately the ocean.
- If you like birds, consider joining a bird conservation program where you track the birds you see in your area. Your records help organisations develop a better understanding of different birds and their habitats.
- Never litter. Pick up any rubbish you see on the beach. Cut back on plastic use, including plastic bags, straws and balloons.
- Plant native trees and other flora.

HERE IS A CAREER!

Ecologists are specialist scientists who survey ecosystems and assess the complex relationships between species in an ecosystem. Ecologists are employed by research institutes, government agencies, conservation groups and environmental trusts. Ecologists are essential in protecting Australia's native species.

Some Organisations That Provide More Information

The Foundation for Australia's Most Endangered Species (FAME)
https://www.fame.org.au/projects

Australian Wildlife Conservancy
http://www.australianwildlife.org

WWF Australia
http://www.wwf.org.au

URBAN HABITATS AND PIT STOPS

You can create places in your garden at home for animals to rest and find sanctuary.

Ways to do this include:

- **adding plants that provide food to your garden.**
- **adding a water feature for birds or frogs.**
- **providing shelter, such as rocks for reptiles or nest boxes for birds.**

JOIN THE CELEBRATION

Australia celebrates National Threatened Species Day annually on 7 September.

FIND OUT MORE

SEARCH KEY WORDS

Forest, woodlands, alpine, subalpine, microhabitats, food chain, food web, extinct, endangered, threatened species, vulnerable species, habitats, conservation, ecosystem, sustainability, biodiversity

SOURCES:

http://www.environment.gov.au
https://www.countryneedspeople.org.au
http://www.gbrmpa.gov.au
http://www.birdlife.org.au
https://www.bushheritage.org.au
http://www.iucnredlist.org
https://www.ehp.qld.gov.au
http://www.australianwildlife.org

Glossary

adaptation: when a species makes changes to help survive their environment
carnivorous: meat eating
climate change: a long-term change in the earth's climate
critical: at a turning point for survival
ecosystem: the living and non-living parts of an area and the interactions between them
endangered: may soon become extinct
endemic: only found in a certain place
extinct: no longer in existence
feral predators: non-native animals that kill and eat other animals
habitat: place where plants and animals live
nocturnal: active at night
recovery plan: a plan for the conservation of a species
rodent: mammals with gnawing teeth such as mice and rats
species: one kind of living thing
threat: anything that may reduce the numbers of a species
threatened: endangered or vulnerable
vulnerable: may soon become endangered
wetlands: areas of land that are temporarily or permanently covered in water

Index